For the Love of God

Dianna Collier

BookLeaf Publishing

India | USA | UK

Presentation by *BookLeaf Publishing*

Web: www.bookleafpub.com

E-mail: info@bookleafpub.com

ISBN: 9789363317291

First edition 2024

Thank you to my best friend Lauren Langwinski for helping me learn the Catholic faith and for being willing to talk about God for hours. To my husband Rick Collier, who supports me during the writing process and is taking this religious journey with me and to Tina Jansen for supporting me and enjoying my writing.

ACKNOWLEDGEMENT

This book is dedicated to God and his church for his Grace and Strength.

PREFACE

During the last several years I went through many hard times. Due to this I turned to God for strength and became Catholic. Through his love and the community at St. John the Evangelist I have found happiness and enjoy dedicating my time to spreading God's word.

Amen I Say

Amen, Amen
I Say, Amen
God is Glory, God is Good
Spread it through the neighborhood

Yell it loud
Through the crowd
Praise God and glory be
For the Lord has saved me

The Son is born
Blow your horn
Believe in him for your sake
Be heaven bound each day you wake

In my heart and in my soul
I will love God until I am old
From far and wide
Tell all why he died

Love the Lord with all your heart
Best way for your day to start
To the Lord I will attend
God Bless and Amen

Glory, Glory, Glory

Glory, Glory, Glory
Tell all his story
To him we all should seek
Both the bold and the meek

Angels in the clouds
Choirs singing to him loud
Worshiping his name and deeds
The sacrifice of hanging on the tree

He sacrificed for us all
The lucky hear his call
See his beauty all around
Hear his voice in the sounds

Defiance and strength shown
Walking into the known
Suffering and death
Losing his last breath

To his father he relied
Till the day he died
Abuse and torture he went through
Dying for me and you

Only Say the Word

At mass it is heard
Only say the word
My soul shall be healed
To him I make my appeal

For the Lord has given us his words
So we can learn his terms
Relieves our concerns
Each receives just deserves

A relationship he is seeking
With the smiling and the weeping
All you need is to believe
Accept the reality

Spirit in our heart and soul
From young to old
He gives us the light
Big and bright

He says 'I am his'
I say 'He is mine'
To each other entwined
To him I am resigned

Loving him through prayer
Helping the poor and needy with care
When life is not fair
I know he will be there

Undefeated

We are not defined by our losses
We are defined by what we survive
Trying to be happy and content
Trying to have hope and strength

Loss can lead to defeat
But God can give release
Will our loss and our sorrow
Bring us a better tomorrow

For on him I depend
For him I will defend
My Lord my belief
Praying to him when I sleep

I can feel him carry me
Helping me to break free
Weak from defeat
Laying my problems at his feet

Knowing in his wisdom
Someday I will see his kingdom
See the shining of his face
Finally finishing the race

Living within his grace
Feeling his loving embrace
Finally with the ones I love
Living in his kingdom above

All His Children

All His Children
Rich or Poor
Lost or Found
Black, White or Brown

Baptist, Lutherans, Catholics
Christians from all demographics
Believing in him we all share
Worshiping him with care

As it says in John 3:16
You just need to believe in me
Jesus gave his life for yours
Everlasting life is through heaven's doors

Good or Bad
Happy or Sad
Single or Married
Young or Widowed

He gives us all the same choice
Let us all rejoice
Listen to his voice
Make the right choice

Questioning Your Faith

Do you believe in Angels
Do you believe in God
Do you believe in Evil
Do you believe in Hell

What happened to your faith
Where has it gone
Why have you walked away
When will you find peace

Do you know God
Do you feel the Holy Spirit
Do you trust in Jesus
Do you want the Trinity

What do you believe
Where do you turn to for support
Why not return to Jesus
When is a man committed

Do miracles happen
Do you believe in fate
Do you pray when times are bad
Do you ask for help when sad

What makes you feel hate
Where do you feel empty
Why do you feel sadness
When do you feel guilt

Do you want baptized with water
Do you want to be fed with bread and wine
Do you want the Holy Spirit to descend
Again, What do you believe

No Light in Sight

A life without God
No chance for beyond
No life ever after
On a path of disaster

No way out
No one to hear you shout
Alone at the end
To late to mend

No inner joy
Life destroyed
Living in darkness
Feeling heartless

To the Devil you are sent
Oh no, not heaven met
It was you who placed you there
As you lived life without a care

Could not even shed for him a tear
This is why you are here
Moaning and crying you will sit
While stuck in a dark pit

If you are reading this you still have time
To gain your faith and train your mind
God is all you really need
For your salvation you should plead

Spreading his Word

A Christian's responsibility
To use our ability
To spread the word
To sing like a bird

Talking about the Lord
I never get bored
Wonderful stories to tell
Like the woman at the well

He saves Jews and Gentiles
Spreading his word for many miles
His words make me smile
Sharing all his trails

He performed many miracles
To the worthy and the criminal
Healing the deaf and the blind
Always being honest and kind

For us he gave his life
Helping others to get it right
You are always in my sight
Making my life bright

Yell from the rooftops
I will never stop
Looking for the lost
Converting at any cost

Glad you are mine
I will meet you at the right time
To you I am confined
With you I am entwined

Peace Unseen

Peace cannot be
It is a reality
War we defend
Men to their death we send

Religion can split society
Causing some anxiety
Hating those different
Being belligerent and ignorant

Money is the root of all evil
Torturing people and causing upheaval
Bullets and bombs are sent
Destruction is meet

At death we are all the same
It is not about fortune and fame
People knowing your name
What you can gain

God can make us whole
He can save our soul
Bring peace to all who seek
To the strong and the weak

Rain to Shine

A warm rainy day
In the middle of May
Rainbow in the sky
God's promise it will dry

Lightning strikes across the clouds
Thunderclaps mighty loud
Winds blow strong
Sounding like a song

God shows his strength
To the human race
Hurricane from the sea
Tornados through the trees

Suddenly the sun shines
So bright it blinds
Sun coming through the sky
Brings a tear to my eye

God's people come out to play
Enjoying it in many ways
Sunny or Grey
Thank you, Lord, for this day

The Trinity

God the Father and Creator
Jesus the Son and Savior
Holy Ghost known to our heart and soul
The Trinity makes us whole

This is what the Catholics believe
Their spirits all working in me
One, Two, Three
Christ made it possible hanging on the tree

Sometimes the holy spirit is forgotten
Until we do something rotten
The spirit is in all of us
In this we can trust

Entwined with me are the three
Feeling me with glee
Giving my life purpose
Not just on the surface

My life to him I give
Through him I will live
Praying he will be there
My life we will share

My Guardian Angel

A guardian angel was assigned to me
After an emergency
I almost lost my life
Permanently closed my eyes

God has a plan
Even though I made him sad
My parents were surprised
I made it out alive

My angel is always there
Watching me with care
Saving me from the unimagined
With me through great sadness

Saved me from the crazy
Watching over me daily
Saved me from a storm
Hoping I will reform

Excitement and misadventure
Roads I have ventured
Always watching, never stopping
Constantly adapting

Thank you, heart and soul
For helping me to get old
When my time comes it will be a relief
As the angel can get some sleep

Suffering

Why do we suffer
Why does he let it happen
Why is there sadness
Why is there sickness

Can there be good without sadness
Can we appreciate our health without sickness
Can we be truly happy without suffering
Can we appreciate life without death

Who can give me strength
Who can give me relief
Who can I trust
Who's words guide me

How do I heal
How do I deal
How do I feel
How do I appeal

The answer to all is the same
Jesus is his name
He is there to carry us
When the going gets tough

He is my salvation
Helps me with my frustration
Even in my grief
I have my belief

He is always there
He is always aware
That I will always care
Loving him through prayer

Tell Me

Learning his word
What occurred
Discovering mystery
Learning the history

Spreading his word to all I know
Telling them he loves them so
The Bible is what I preach
Trying to spread my reach

Explaining his declarations
Giving them explanations
Relieving them of their doubt
Learning what it is all about

Who should have their loyalty
Who can stop the cruelty
Who can save their soul
Who to turn to when you get old

Telling them how you adore
Loving the Lord
Giving you sweet relief
From sorrow and grief

On him you can depend
My prayers to him I send
Telling all my friends
That their lives he can mend

All they need is to believe
That he can set them free
Everlasting life he offers
To his sons and daughters

The Clouds

Glimpses of heaven seen in the clouds
Familiar faces staring down
Checking up and watching me
Hope they like what they see

Dragon in the sky
Looking through watchful eyes
Head large and scaly
Tail long and wavy

Stairway through the clouds
Waterfall built of little mounds
Lovely cascading down
Moving without sound

Look at the bear
Chasing the hare
Mother with her son
Man holding a gun

It is what your mind perceives
On the images you receive
It tells a lot about the inner me
What will be, will be

For the Love of Jesus

Jesus selected those from Galilee
To be treated as family
Even though they go happily
It will end in calamity

His birth changed the earth
His worth is shown in the church
At times what you hear
Will make you shed a tear

In his embrace
You will find grace
For all the human race
So they can see his face

In the past they would slaughter
Now they bless with water
All your sins will depart
Ask for forgiveness in your heart

His life was taken by force
His body hung on the cross
His innocents we disregarded
Being heckled by the guards

Jesus prayed for compassion
As he went through the passion
Praying for unity
Within the Jewish community

It is important to believe in the Lord
Walk through heaven's door
For those that believe
You will be received

We are all in his hands
If you follow his commands
It takes time to understand
You are part of his plan

Why the Mystery

Why is it a mystery
When is it contradictory
The Lord My God does exist
The truth is hard to resist

The proof is all around
His presence in every sound
Keeping everything bound
Earth his glorious crown

Smiling at us from the moon
Humming in tune
Winking at us through the stars
Playing strings on guitars

Earth provides us food
Rain provides water
Sun provides warmth
Night provides us rest

Soil provide growth
Plants provides seed
Seeds provides vegetables
Foods provides us life

Needs provided by the cow
Nutrients for milk
Protein from meat
Protection from leather

Everything has a purpose
Built into its circuits
Winter and Summer
Relaying on each other

Mystery uncovered
Life discovered
Feel him in my soul
Reassurance when I get old

Only fools don't believe
Just because they cannot see
I know he will set me free
A life eternal for me

The Ultimate Question

What is the ultimate question
That gives us all tension
It gives us all a connection
Has our complete attention

What will happen when we die
Is there a heaven in the sky
Was I told a lie
That will make me cry

Am I right with the Lord
Will I get my reward
Did I have self-control
Do I have a clean soul

Did I pray the rosary
Write him some poetry
Was my record smudged
Will I be misjudged

Is there a pit underneath
With moaning and gashing of teeth
What is your story
How did you end up in purgatory

With my daily confession
Giving up possession
Living on earth
Giving to his church

Worshipping his birth
Experiencing my rebirth
He is mine
On him I can rely

Taking his bread and wine
Honoring the divine
For he is pure
Everlasting life he will secure

Purgatory

Purgatory is what you need
To make yourself clean
Burning off all your sin
Be holy so heaven will let you in

To see the light of God's face
But not able to embrace
To except the sins you denied
Until the day you died

Please pray for me
To be relieved of agony
So I can enter the light
Set everything right

People of earth don't forget about me
When you pray the rosary
Mother Mary please intercede
Forgiveness and understanding are what I need

You did commit moral sins
Would not let God in
Confession you should have seeked
Spoken to a Catholic priest

Evil and temptation will deceive
As your soul the devil tried to receive
To the Lord you must return
His word you need to learn

Purgatory is not a place
It is your soul laid to waste
Where you examine your soul
You finally feel the toll

Church you should have attended
God you have offended
Holy the Sabbath should be kept
Give to your neighbor till nothing left

Goods and gold mean nothing
When the final bell rings
Want to hear the angels sing
For the heavenly king

The 10 commandments you did not obey
Did not listen to what the bible says
Earthly possession and wealth
Only thinking of yourself

May your time be short
As you go through court
May you submit to him your soul
Until you are truly whole

The Last Days

There are many prophecies
Depending on what one believes
The Christ will come again
Bring our suffering to an end

Peace on earth
A spiritual rebirth
On a cloud he will descend
It will be much to comprehend

From this life I will be free
Because he died for me
All my sins forgiven
As my confessions were given

Depending on your story
You may go to purgatory
Jesus will speak on my behalf
When others attack

For those who are weak, he will lead
For those who are hungry, he will feed
For those who are lost, he will find
For those who love him, he will bind

So happy I will be
When he comes for me
Finally to be with him
Listening to the hymns

At the Pearly Gates

As I stand at the pearly gates
Awaiting my fate
Shaking with fear
Eyes full of tears

I could feel Jesus was near
Relieving all my fear
Why do you have tears
When you are welcome here

The light shown around his face
Smiling at me full of grace
My daughter I am glad you are here
Thank you for keeping me near

I did not know what to say
I always welcomed this day
For this is where I want to stay
Living my life his way

Jesus extended his hand
Knowing he will understand
Lose of all my grief
Feeling happiness in my belief

A city of brilliant glass and light
Shining so bright
Temple of God in sight
Trembling with delight

The Lord hugged me
My family was in front of me
My dogs and cats running to me
No happier could I be